Kites

Fiona Macdonald

Oxford

Oxford University Press, Great Clarendon Street, Oxford, OX2 6DP

Oxford New York
Athens Auckland Bangkok Bogota Buenos Aires
Calcutta Cape Town Chennai Dar es Salaam Delhi
Florence Hong Kong Istanbul Karachi Kuala Lumpur
Madrid Melbourne Mexico City Mumbai Nairobi Paris
São Paulo Singapore Taipei Tokyo Toronto Warsaw

and associated companies in
Berlin Ibadan

Oxford is a trade mark of Oxford University Press

Text © Fiona Macdonald 1999
Published by Oxford University Press 1999
A CIP record for this book is available from the British Library

ISBN 0 19 915592 5
Available in packs
Toys Pack of Six (one of each book)   ISBN 0 19 915595 X
Toys Class Pack   (six of each book)   ISBN 0 19 915617 4

Printed in Hong Kong

Acknowledgements

The publisher would like to thank the following for permission to reproduce photographs:

Art Directors Photo Library p 10 (*left*); Barnabys Picture Library p 4; Camera Ways p 15 (*left*); Colorific pp 3, 12 (*left*), 15, 17 (*left*); Corbis UK p 12; Flexifoil p 13; Getty Images /Tony Stone Worldwide p 5; J. Allan Cash pp 10 (right), 13 (*left*); Kite Society of Great Britain p 6; National Meteorological Library p 18 (*left*); Pictor International pp 5 (*left* and *centre*), 16, 17; Science and Society Picture Library p 18 (*right* and *centre*); Science Photo Library / J. Stevenson p 21; Skyscan p 10 (*centre*).

Illustrations by Peter Bull Art Studio pp 11, 14, 22, 23; Lesley Smith pp 7, 8, 9, 20; Annabel Spenceley pp 19, 21.

Front cover photograph Telegraph Colour Library.
Back cover photograph Corbis UK.

Contents

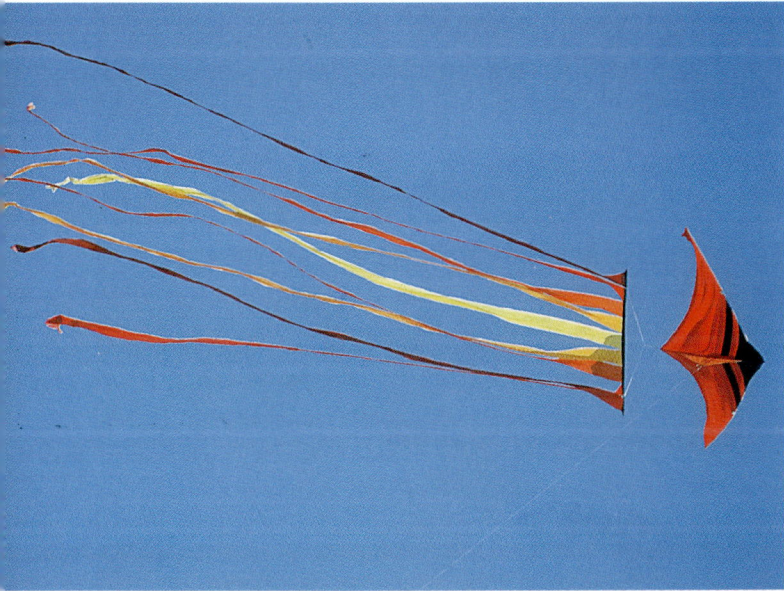

Introduction

Kites are simple
flying machines.
They are fixed
to long strings.
You hold the
string while the
kite flies in the sky.

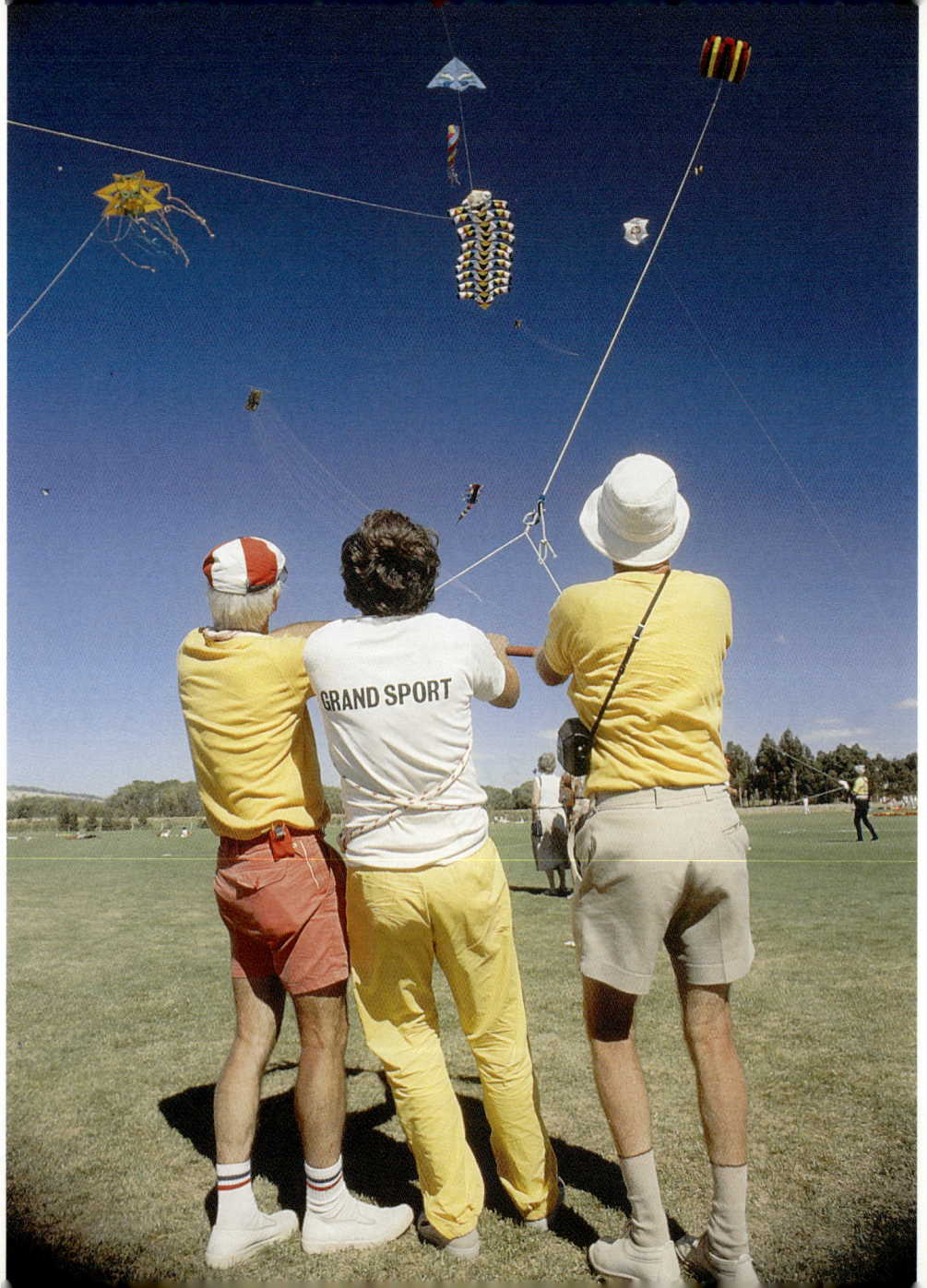

Some kites are toys, but there are many different kinds of kites. This book will tell you about some of them.

The first kites

People have made kites for thousands of years.
The first kites were made in China and Japan.

No-one knows how kites
were invented.

Kites might have been
invented when people
saw how leaves blew
in the wind.

They might have been
invented when people's
hats blew around in the
wind.

How a kite flies

Kites fly when the wind blows them.

To make a kite fly you need to run into the wind. ▶

wind

◀ The wind blows against the kite and lifts it up into the air.

wind

wind

wind

The wind pushes from underneath and keeps the kite up in the air.

If the wind stops blowing, the kite falls to the ground.

Kite design

Kites are made in many shapes and sizes.

Flat kites fly fast. ▼

Tube-shaped kites catch the wind well. The wind blows through the tube. ▼

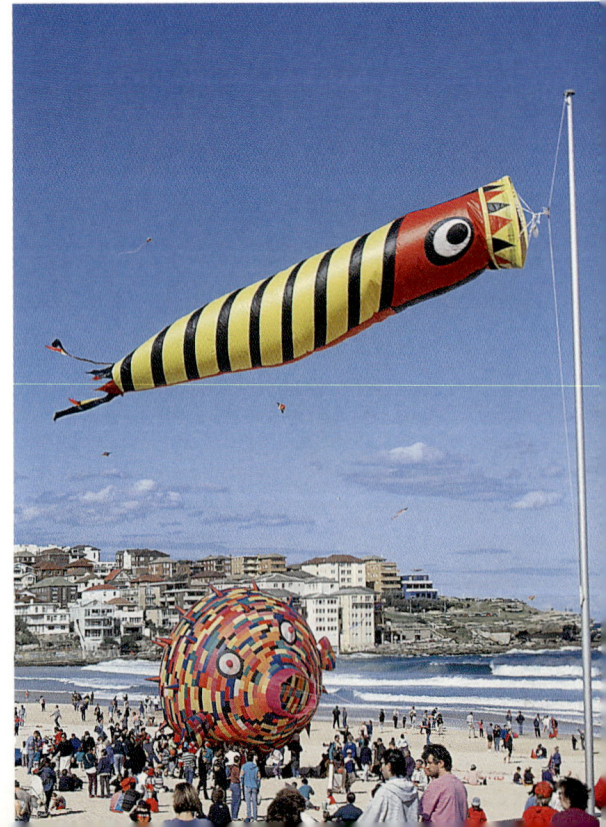

▲ Box-shaped kites are very strong.

Most kites have a cover and a frame. Most kites have a tail, too.

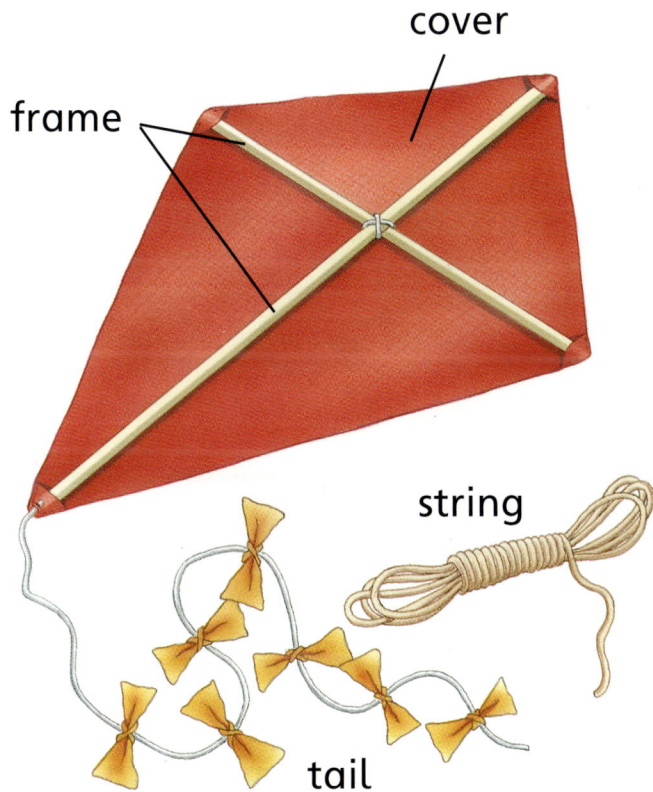

cover

frame

string

tail

Materials for making kites have to be light and strong.

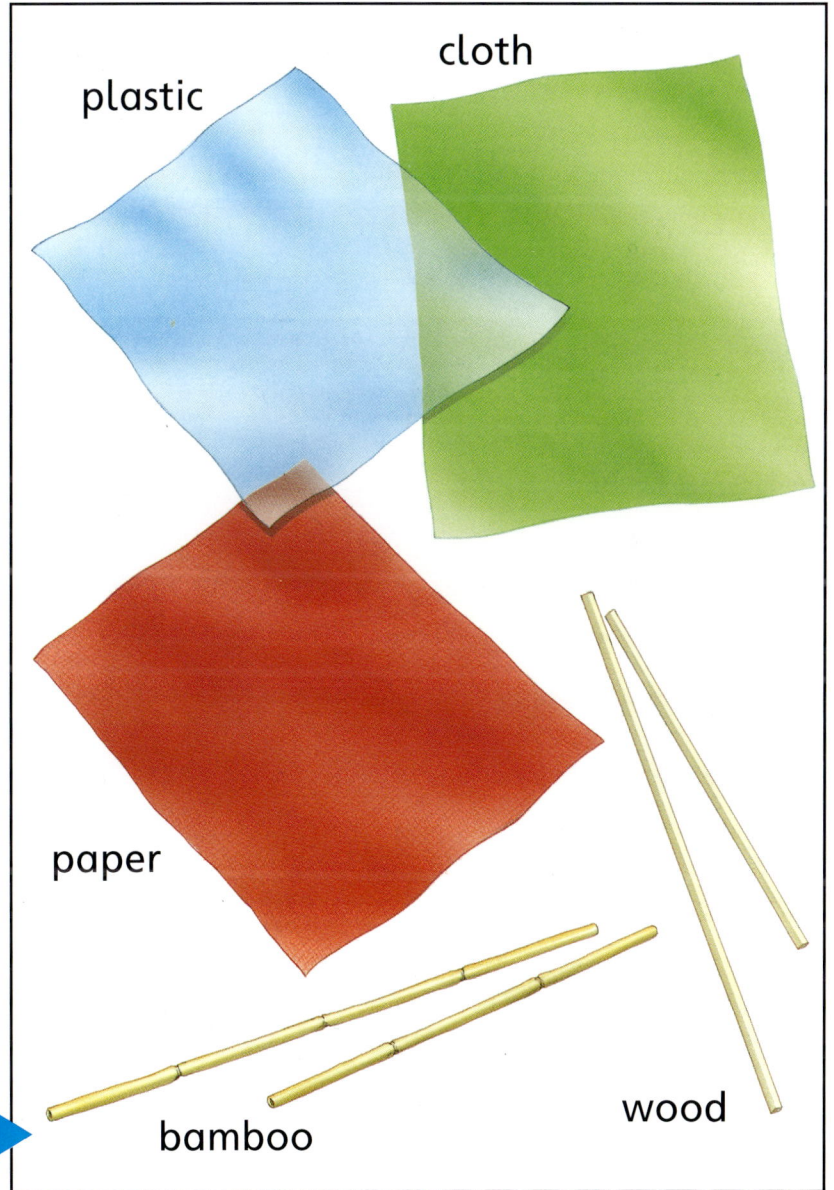

plastic

cloth

paper

bamboo

wood

Kites for sport

Kites are often used for sports.

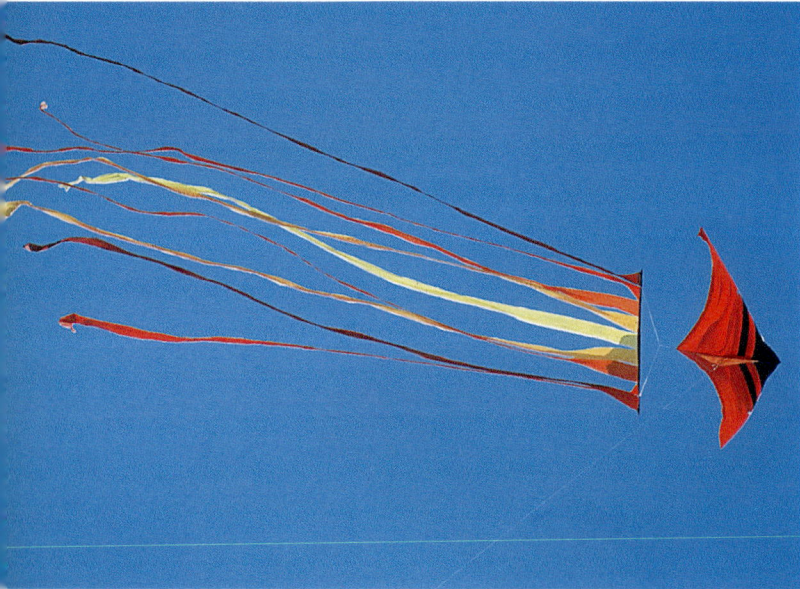

Giant kites need lots of people to fly them. They can fly at 60 miles an hour. ▼

Stunt kites swoop and dive. ▲
They sometimes need two strings
to control them.

These people are having a kite flying competition. ▼

▲

This man is being pulled along the beach by a power kite.

Fighting kites

In some countries, people make fighting kites. The kites have pieces of metal tied to their strings.

1 People fly the kites towards each other. ▶

◀ **2** People try to make their kites cut other kites' strings.

Fighting kites fly
very fast.

◀ These fighting
kites are in
Bristol.

Kite festivals

There are kite festivals in many parts of the world.

▲ In Japan, people fly fish kites for their children. They hope the children will grow up to be strong, like the fish.

In India, people fly star-shaped kites in springtime. They hope the kites will bring good weather.

Kites for lifting

These old kites carried instruments to measure the weather.

Big, strong kites can even carry people.

This kite was designed in 1902. It could carry one person.

Kites for different sorts of work

Kites have always been used for work.

Fishermen used kites to carry fishing lines out into the water. ▼

Soldiers used kites to frighten their enemies.

Nowadays, pilots use wind-sock kites to help them see which way the wind is blowing.

Make your own kite

You will need these materials to make your kite.

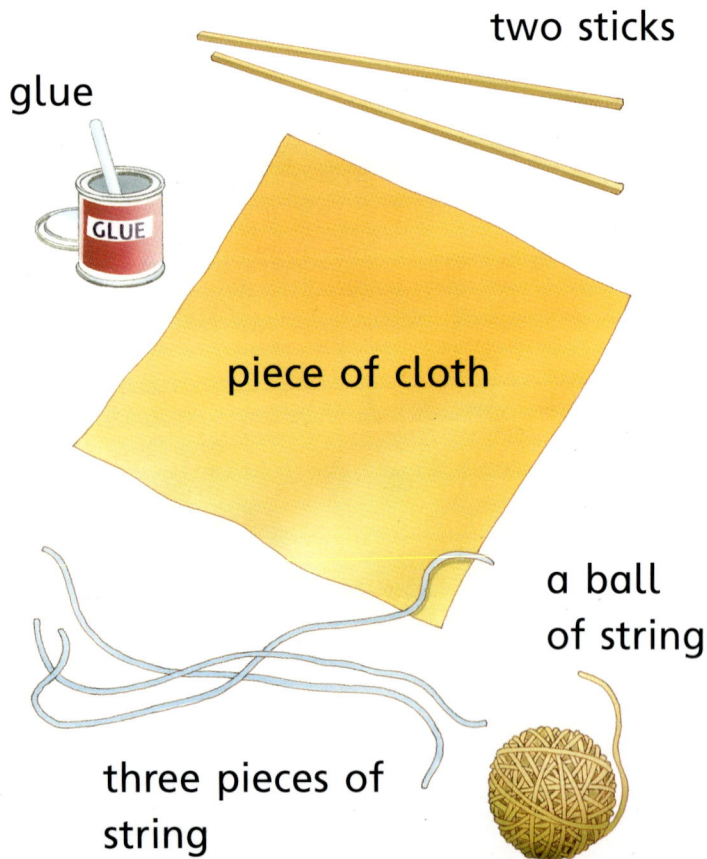

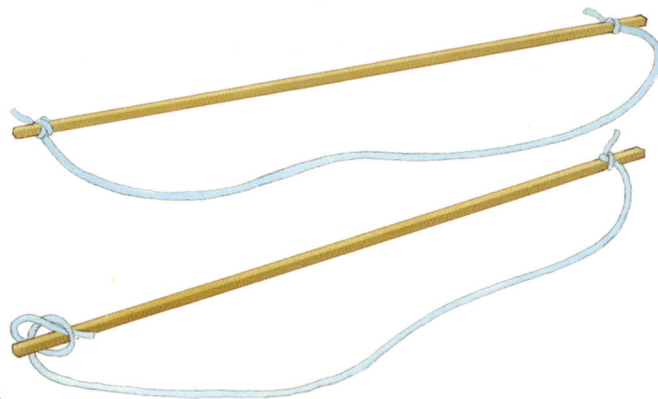

two sticks

glue

GLUE

piece of cloth

a ball of string

three pieces of string

1 Tie two of the pieces of string to the ends of the sticks, like this.

2 Cut the corners off the cloth, and glue down the sides.

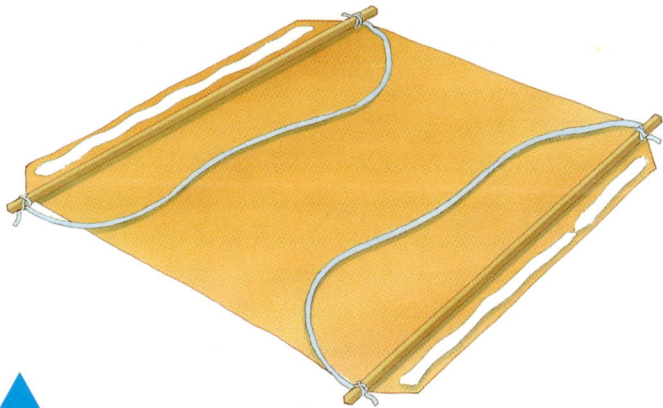

3 Lay the sticks on the edges of the cloth.

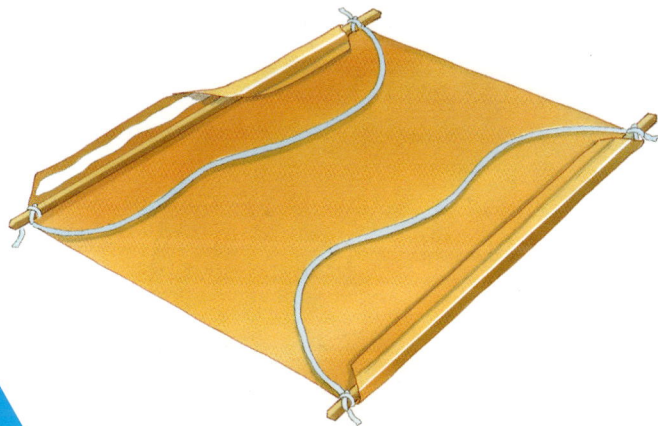

4 Fold the cloth over the sticks.

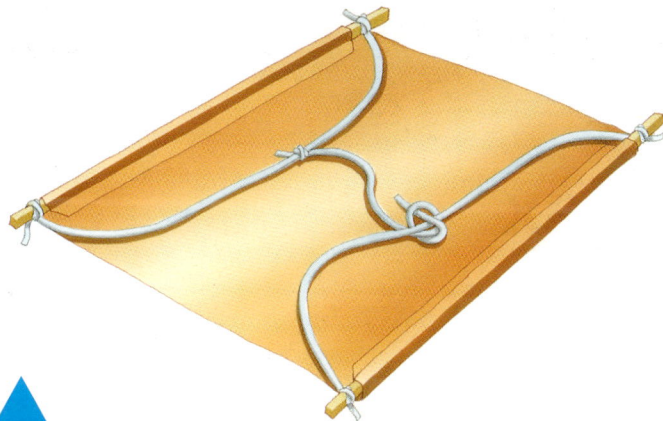

5 Tie the third piece of string to the other two pieces, like this.

6 Tie the ball of string to the third piece, like this.

Index

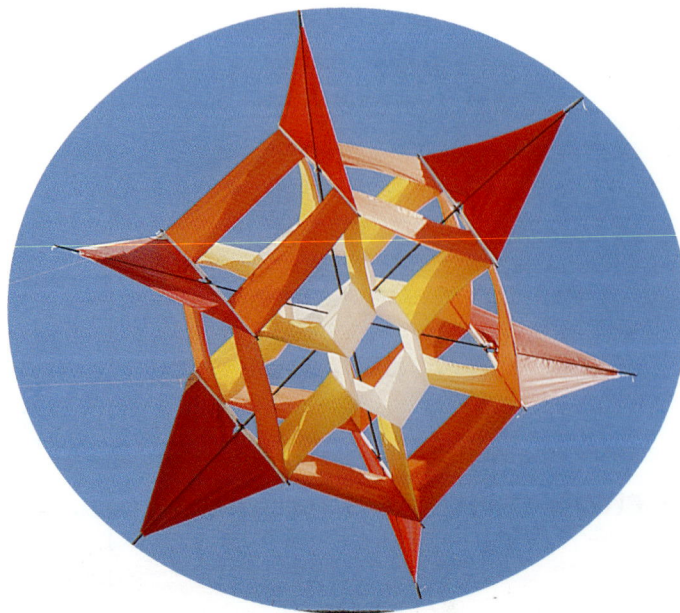